DASH DIET COOKBOOK

Yummy

Dash Diet Receipes, Dash Diet Eating Plan for a Happy Healthy Life

Table of Contents

Introduction 4

Chapter 1 5

    DASH Diet - Real-Life Solutions 5

    5 Benefits of a DASH Diet - Proven to Lower Your Blood Pressure .. 7

    What Makes The DASH Diet Different? 8

    How to Reduce Sodium Intake 9

Chapter 2 12

    7 Advisable Foods While on a DASH Diet - Save Your Body From High Blood Pressure 12

    Foods To Avoid On The DASH Diet. 14

    The Steps Involved in Following the DASH Diet 15

Chapter 3: 72 Delicious DASH Diet Recipes 16

    1. Breakfast Recipes 16

    2. Lunch Recipes 58

    3. Dinner Recipes 97

    4. Desserts Recipes 137

Conclusion 162

Introduction

DASH stands for Dietary Approach to Stop Hypertension. DASH diet has been clinically proven to reduce blood pressure within 2 weeks in individuals following the diet. It is not only known to help manage the blood pressure but is also designed for weight loss programs, helps to prevent heart diseases, stroke, diabetes and some forms of cancer. DASH was developed by the United States National Heart, Lung and Blood Institute (NHLBI).

Hypertension, or high blood pressure, affects more than 65 million Americans. This means a staggering proportion of 1 out of 3 Americans. There are also 59 million Americans who are said to have prehypertension or borderline hypertension.

When blood courses through the blood vessels at abnormally high pressures, the arterial walls harden, the heart works so hard and the delicately tiny vessels in the brain, eyes, heart, and kidneys may rupture and hemorrhage to cause stroke, blindness, heart attack, and kidney failure. The optimum blood pressure should be 120/80 mm Hg. A blood pressure of 120/80 to 140/89 is already prehypertension while blood pressure of 140/90 and higher is full-blown hypertension.

DASH diet has been shown to prevent and lower blood pressure. For effective results, one should follow the DASH diet in conjunction with:

- ✓ moderate physical activity for at least 30 minutes each day on most days of the week
- ✓ maintaining a healthy weight, and
- ✓ moderation, if not abstinence, from alcohol.

Chapter 1
DASH Diet - Real-Life Solutions

This diet, coined as the 'Healthiest Diet', is designed to provide real-life solutions to high blood pressure by suggesting a diet that merely regulates the intake of nutrients and not alters the common diet we're all used to. Dietary Approaches to Stop Hypertension or dash focuses on controlling the intake of sodium and fats to maintain the normal blood pressure of an individual. Dash is geared towards preparing a diet that makes satisfying meals, thus, preventing people from eating in-between meals, causing loss of control over food intake. Because it keeps people from hunger in-between meals, it ideally becomes more satisfying and less controlling.

The Dash diet teaches individuals to complete the whole dash diet program by starting with stocking up the kitchen with dash-friendly food, preparing dash-friendly recipes, and performing Dash-friendly exercises. Meal plans suggested by Dash usually contain ingredients high in fiber, calcium, magnesium, and potassium. Dash diets go low on sodium and sugar and emphasize the need to eat green leafy vegetables and fruits.

Avocado dip, for instance, is one of the most famous Dash diets there today due to its very convenient and affordable preparation. Avocado, a very rich source of monosaturated fat and lutein, (antioxidants that help protect vision), is among the many fruits that are highly recommended for the Dash diet. In this recipe, avocado has to be mashed and pitted, mixed with fat-free sour cream, onion, and hot sauce. This dip shall be eaten with tortilla chips or sliced vegetables. From this dish, a person can get a total of 65 calories, 2 grams protein, 5 grams total fat, 4 grams carbohydrate, 172 milligrams potassium and 31 milligrams calcium. From this, we can infer that a person is fed a considerable amount of necessary nutrients, essential for maintaining a well-balanced diet that's good for the heart.

In just 14 days, a Dash diet follower will experience normal blood pressure, with fewer tendencies to eat in-between meals, the major culprit of weight gain. The Dash diet program also teaches individuals to determine the right amount of food intake, the necessary exercise to perform according to age and activity level. Dash educates and motivates - one of the very important reasons why people find it easy to stick to the diet. Also, the diet does not require us to give up anything significant in our usual diet, instead, it helps us create a process of adjusting to little changes so we can successfully help ourselves.

5 Benefits of a DASH Diet - Proven to Lower Your Blood Pressure

DASH has five benefits to offer if followed strictly. First, overall fat, saturated fat, and cholesterol levels are reduced. Heart attack, stroke, and other cardiovascular diseases are also prevented.

Second, the increased intake of fruits, vegetables, and low-fat dairy foods also increases lycopene, beta-carotene, and phytochemicals in the body. Phytochemicals help protect the body from cancers and heart diseases, and they can be found in plants.

Third, fiber intake is increased by including whole grain products in the plan. Fiber aids in the digestion of food and the lessening of cholesterol levels as well.

Fourth, the reduction of sodium in one's diet to no more than 1,500 milligrams a day can be an effective treatment for hypertension. The lesser the salt intake, the lower the blood pressure becomes. Thus, the risks of atherosclerosis and congestive heart failure are lessened.

Fifth, sweets and beverages high in sugar are avoided. This helps one to lower calorie intake and maintains sugar balance in the body.

In summary, DASH diet is loaded with minerals like magnesium, potassium, calcium, and protein. It doesn't only lower sodium and cholesterol in the body, but it also provides the needed major body nutrients.

What Makes The DASH Diet Different?

The DASH diet focuses its attention on what you should be eating, rather than on what you should not be eating, and at its simplest recommends eating a balance of fruit and vegetables supplemented with some low-fat dairy products.

Fruits and vegetables are excellent diet products (as long as you eat a range of both and don't simply limit yourself to just one or two of your favorite fruits and vegetables) for two main reasons.

First, fruit and vegetables have high water content and are low in calories. This means that you do not need to eat large quantities to feel full. Similarly, large quantities will not provide a high-calorie intake.

Second, fruit and vegetables provide not only your necessary daily intake of fiber but are also high in essential vitamins and minerals which are essential to keeping you healthy while you are dieting.

How to Reduce Sodium Intake

The DASH diet is very low in sodium (Sodium plays a significant role in hypertension). 70 % of the sodium we consume, comes from packaged and restaurant foods. That can make it hard to control how much sodium you take because it's added to your food before you buy it. Here are some basic tips to help you minimize your sodium intake.

1. At The Store/While Shopping For Food

• Choose packaged and prepared foods carefully. Compare labels and choose the product with the lowest amount of sodium (per serving) you can find in your store. You might be surprised that different brands of the same food can have different sodium levels.

• Pick fresh and frozen poultry that hasn't been injected with a sodium solution. Check the fine print on the packaging for terms like "broth," "saline" or "sodium solution." Sodium levels in unseasoned fresh meats are around 100 milligrams (mg) or less per 4-ounce serving.

• Select condiments with care. For example, soy sauce, bottled salad dressings, dips, ketchup, jarred salsas, capers, mustard, pickles, olives, and relish can be sky-high in sodium. Look for a reduced- or lower-sodium version.

• Opt for canned vegetables labeled "no salt added" and frozen vegetables without salty sauces. When they're added to a casserole, soup or other mixed dishes, there are so many other ingredients involved that you won't miss the salt.

- Look for products with the American Heart Association's Heart-Check mark to find foods that can be part of an overall healthy dietary pattern.

2. When Preparing Food

- Use onions, garlic, herbs, spices, citrus juices and vinegars in place of some or all of the salt to add flavor. Our recipes and tips can help!

- Drain and rinse canned beans (like chickpeas, kidney beans, etc.) and vegetables. You'll cut the sodium by up to 40 percent.

- Combine lower-sodium versions of food with regular versions. If you don't like the taste of lower-sodium foods right now, try combining them in equal parts with a regular version of the same food. You'll get less salt and probably won't notice much difference in taste. This works especially well for broths, soups and tomato-based pasta sauces.

- Cook pasta, rice and hot cereal without salt. You're likely going to add other flavorful ingredients, so you won't miss the salt.

- Cook by grilling, braising, roasting, searing and sautéing to bring out natural flavors. This will reduce the need to add salt.

- Incorporate foods with potassium like sweet potatoes, potatoes, greens, tomatoes, and lower-sodium tomato sauce, white beans, kidney beans, nonfat yogurt, oranges, bananas, and cantaloupe. Potassium helps counter the effects of sodium and may help lower your blood pressure.

3. At restaurants

- Tell them how you like it. Ask for your dish to be made without extra salt.

- Taste your food before adding salt. If you think it needs a boost of flavor, add freshly ground black pepper or a squeeze of fresh lemon or lime and test it again before adding salt. Lemon and pepper are especially good on fish, chicken, and vegetables.

- Watch out for these food words: pickled, brined, barbecued, cured, smoked, broth, soy sauce, miso or teriyaki sauce. These tend to be high in sodium. Foods that are steamed, baked, grilled, poached or roasted may have less sodium.

- Control portion sizes. When you cut calories, you usually cut the sodium too. Ask if smaller portions are available, share the meal with a friend or ask for a to-go box when you order and place half the meal in the box to eat later.

Chapter 2
7 Advisable Foods While on a DASH Diet - Save Your Body From High Blood Pressure

1. Foods enriched with whole grains like bread, oatmeal, cereals, pasta, and rice. Grains provide good sources of energy for the body.

2. Fruits and Vegetables - These two foods are recommended for everyday intake, at least eight to ten servings a day. Tomatoes, carrots, broccoli, sweet potatoes as well as oranges, apples, and prunes, are rich in fiber, protein, carbohydrates, vitamins, and minerals.

3. Dairy Products - Milk, yogurt and cheese are three main dairy entrees containing major vitamins, calcium, and protein. Fat-free or low-fat dairy products are effective during DASH reduction.

4. Meat, Poultry, and Fish - Meat and fish, either processed or raw, are a rich source of proteins, vitamin B, iron and zinc. Prepare and cook it properly by taking the skin and fats before either broiling, roasting or frying.

5. Nuts, Seeds, and Beans - Almonds, kidney beans and sunflower seeds and the like are good sources of magnesium, potassium and protein. They are also rich in fiber and its phytochemicals help fight against cancers and cardiovascular diseases.

6. Low-fat Sweets - Jellybeans, graham crackers and light flavored cookies are also considered for consumption in this program. Dark

chocolate is also recommended since it contains substances that lower hypertension.

7. Low-sodium snacks - Buy nourishments which has "no salt added" or "low sodium-rich" trademarks found in bold parts of the snack.

Foods To Avoid On The DASH Diet.

The DASH diet limits foods that will negatively impact your blood pressure and heart health. The following foods should be avoided when following the eating plan.

- ✓ *High-sodium foods*

Studies have shown that drastically cutting back on dietary salt is associated with decreased risk of hypertension, heart disease, and stroke. Not sprinkling salt on your meals is one of the biggest challenges followers of the DASH diet face. However, salt reduction is integral to the plan, so opt for herbs and spices instead.

Sources of high sodium include; Table salt, Fast food, Pre-packaged food, Processed meats.

- ✓ *Red meats*

The DASH diet emphasizes fish and chicken over red meat. Though it's not strictly forbidden, red meat consumption should be limited since it's high in saturated fat and cholesterol. Sources red meat include: Beef, Pork, Lamb & Veal.

- ✓ *Saturated fat*

The DASH diet recommends reducing your intake of foods high in saturated fat. Sources of saturate fats include: Cheese, Fatty cuts of meat, Poultry with skin, Lard, Cream, Butter &Whole milk.

The Steps Involved in Following the DASH Diet

The first step involved before embarking on the DASH Diet is determining your Daily Caloric Needs. This is quite easy as you only have to key in your age and your level of physical activity and refer to a chart.

Once you have the figure for your Daily Calorie Needs, the second step would be to refer to the DASH eating plan chart and just look for the closest calorie level to yours. This step basically tells you how many servings of each food group you are allowed to take in every day so you can change your eating pattern.

Chapter 3: 72 Delicious DASH Diet Recipes

1. Breakfast Recipes

Lime Chicken Tacos

Total Time: 6 hrs 30 Minutes

Yield: 6 servings.

Ingredients

- 1-1/2 pounds boneless skinless chicken breast halves
- 3 tablespoons lime juice
- Lime zest
- 1 tablespoon chili powder
- 1 cup frozen corn, thawed
- 1 cup chunky salsa
- 12 fat-free flour tortillas (6 inches), warmed

Optional : Sour cream, jalapenos, shredded lettuce, or your favorite 2% Mexican shredded cheese

Directions

Place chicken in a 3-qt. slow cooker. Combine lime juice and chili powder; pour over chicken.

Then cook, covered, on low until chicken is tender, 5-6 hours.

Remove chicken. When cool enough to handle, shred meat with two forks; return to slow cooker. Stir in corn and salsa.

Then cook, covered, on low until heated through, about 30 minutes. Place filling on tortillas; or crispy tacos and add some of your favorite condiments like lite sour cream, jalapenos, lettuce and cheese.

Quinoa & Squash Casserole

Total Time: 4 Hours

Yield: 10 servings

Ingredients

- 12 ounces tomatillos, Mexican husked tomatoes, rinsed and chopped
- 1-pint cherry tomatoes, chopped
- 1 red bell pepper, chopped
- ½ cup finely chopped white onion
- 1 tablespoon lime juice
- 1 cup quinoa
- 1 cup crumbled low sodium gruyere or Swiss cheese, divided

- 2 pounds small yellow summer squash, cut into ¼-inch slices
- 2 tablespoons chopped fresh oregano

Directions

Combine tomatillos, tomatoes, pepper, onion, lime juice and salt in a medium bowl.

Spray your 5- to 6-quart slow cooker with cooking spray.

Layer quinoa, ⅓ cup cheese and all of the squash in the slow cooker. Top with another ⅓ cup cheese. Spread the tomatillo mixture on top, but don't stir the ingredients together. (Refrigerate the remaining cheese to use for the topping.)

Cover and cook on Low for 4 hours. Serve sprinkled with oregano and the remaining ⅓ cup cheese.

Coconut Quinoa Curry

Total Time: 3 - 4 Hours

Serves: 6

Ingredients

- 1 medium sweet potato, peeled + chopped (about 3 cups)
- 2 cups of fresh green beans (cut into ½ inch pieces)
- 1 medium-size carrot (cut into small bite-size pieces)
- ½ white onion, diced (about 1 cup)
- 1 (15 oz) can organic chickpeas, drained and rinsed
- 1 (28 oz) can diced tomatoes
- 2 (14.5 oz) cans coconut milk (either full fat or lite)
- ¼ cup quinoa
- 2 garlic cloves, minced (about 1 tablespoon)
- 1 tablespoon freshly grated ginger

- 1 tablespoon freshly grated turmeric (or 1 teaspoon ground)
- 2 teaspoon tamari sauce
- ½ - 1 teaspoon chili flakes
- 1 - 1½ cups of water

Instructions

Add all ingredients to a slow cooker, starting with 1 cup of water. Stir until everything is fully incorporated.

Turn the slow cooker to high and cook for 3 - 4 hours until sweet potato cooks through and the curry has thickened.

You can serve as is like a vegetarian soup or on balsamic rice.

Black Bean Chili

Total Cook Time: 6-8 Hours

Serves: 4

Ingredients

- 1 1/2 cups bell pepper (any color), chopped
- 1 1/2 cups white mushrooms, sliced
- 1 cup onion, chopped
- 1 tbsp olive oil
- 2 garlic cloves, finely chopped
- 1 tbsp chili powder
- 1 tsp canned chipotle chili, chopped
- 1/2 tsp cumin
- 1 can (15.5 oz) can low-sodium black beans, rinsed and drained

- 1 cup diced tomatoes, canned no-salt-added
- 2 tbsp cilantro, chopped

Directions

Combine all the ingredients into your Crockpot

Cook on High for 4 hours and let it simmer until you are ready to eat.

Or if you are going out, cook on low for 6-8 hours and then let it simmer.

Slow cookeer Chicken With Potatoes

Total Cook Time:4 Hours

Serves: 4

Ingredients

- 1.5- 2 lbs Boneless Skinless Chicken Breasts
- ½ lb. fresh green beans, trimmed (about 2.5 cups)
- 1.25 lb. diced red potatoes (about 4 cups)
- ⅓ cup FRESH lemon juice
- ¼ cup olive oil
- 1 tsp. dried oregano

- 1 tsp. dried cilantro
- ¼ tsp. pepper
- ¼ tsp. onion powder
- 2 garlic cloves, minced

Instructions

Start by placing the chicken in a 6-quart crockpot, in the center. Next, add the green beans on one side. Then for the potatoes, you will need to mound them high off to the other side.

In a medium-sized bowl, whisk together the lemon juice, olive oil, oregano, cilantro, pepper, onion powder, and garlic cloves.

Pour this mixture evenly over the chicken, green beans and potatoes.

Cover and cook on HIGH for 4 hours, without opening the lid during the cooking time.

Note- Do NOT use lemon juice out of the squeeze bottle and expect this to taste good.

Mashed Potatoes

Total Time: 30 Min

Yield: 10 servings

Ingredients

- 5 lb russet potato, peeled and cut into large chunks
- cold water
- 1 tablespoon kosher salt, plus more to taste
- 8 tablespoons unsalted butter, cubed
- 1 cup heavy cream
- ½ cup whole milk
- freshly ground black pepper, to taste

- 1 tablespoon fresh chives, chopped, for garnish

Directions

Place the potatoes in a large pot and cover with cold water. Add the salt. Bring to a boil over high heat and cook until the potatoes are fork-tender, about 20 minutes longer.

Drain the potatoes and press through a potato ricer into a large bowl. Set aside.

Heat the butter, cream, and milk in a small pot over low heat until simmering.

Pour the cream mixture over the potatoes and stir to combine. Season to taste with salt and pepper.

Garnish with chives, if desired.

Enjoy!

Apple Crisp

Total Cook Time:4 Hours

Yield:6 servings

Ingredients

- 1 Cup oatmeal
- 1 cup brown sugar
- 2 tablespoon of all-purpose flour
- 1 tablespoon granulated sugar
- 1 stick of butter
- 1 teaspoon cinnamon
- 3 lbs Granny Smith Apples

Instructions

Peel and core apples and thinly slice. Add granulated sugar and flour to the apples and toss to coat. Place Apples into the bottom of a 5-6 quart crockpot.

Mix brown sugar, oatmeal and butter until you have a crumbly mixture and then sprinkle oatmeal mixture on top of the apples.

Cook on HIGH for 4 hours or until apples are fully cooked.

If you prefer peaches here is a Peach Cobbler Recipe made with frozen peaches.

Overnight Oats

Total Cook Time:6 Hrs 5 Min

Yield:1 Serving

Ingredients

Oats

- 1/2 cup unsweetened plain almond milk (or sub other dairy-free glasses of milk, such as coconut, soy, or hemp!)
- 3/4 Tbsp chia seeds
- 2 Tbsp natural salted peanut butter or almond butter (creamy or crunchy // or sub other nut or seed butter)
- 1 Tbsp maple syrup (or sub coconut sugar, organic brown sugar, or stevia to taste)

- 1/2 cup gluten-free rolled oats (rolled oats are best, vs. steel-cut or quick-cooking)

Toppings - Optional

- Sliced banana, strawberries, or raspberries
- Flaxseed meal or additional chia seed
- Granola

Instructions

To a mason jar or small bowl with a lid, add almond milk, chia seeds, peanut butter, and maple syrup (or other sweeteners) and stir with a spoon to combine. The peanut butter doesn't need to be completely mixed with the almond milk (doing so leaves swirls of peanut butter to enjoy the next day).

Add oats and stir a few more times. Then press down with a spoon to ensure all oats have been moistened and are immersed in almond milk.

Cover securely with a lid or seal and set in the refrigerator overnight (or for at least 6 hours) to set/soak.

The next day, open and enjoy as is or garnish with desired toppings (see options above).

OPTIONAL: You can also heat your oats in the microwave for 45-60 seconds (just ensure there's enough room at the top of your jar to allow for expansion and prevent overflow), or transfer oats to a saucepan and heat over medium heat until warmed through. Add more liquid as needed if oats get too thick/dry.

Overnight oats will keep in the refrigerator for 2-3 days, though best within the first 12-24 hours in our experience. Not freezer friendly.

Muesli Scones

Total Time: 35 Min

Yield:16 servings

Ingredients

- 2 cups self-raising flour
- 1/2 cup plain flour
- 1 tablespoon caster sugar
- 30g butter, chilled, chopped
- 3/4 cup milk
- 3/4 cup toasted muesli
- Butter, to serve
- Honey, to serve

Directions

Preheat oven to 250°C. Lightly grease a 19cm square (base) cake pan.

Sift flours and sugar into a large bowl. Add butter. Using fingertips, rub the butter into the flour until the mixture resembles breadcrumbs. Add milk. Using a flat-bladed knife, stir to form a soft dough, adding more milk if necessary. Turn dough onto a lightly floured surface. Add muesli. Knead gently until dough comes together.

Cut dough in half. Shape 1 half of dough into a 2cm-thick round. Using a 5cm scone cutter or glass, cut rounds from dough. Repeat with dough scraps. Place scones in prepared pan. Repeat with remaining dough and dough scraps.

Bake scones for 12 to 15 minutes or until golden. Serve with butter and honey.

Breakfast Cookies

Total Time: 25 Minutes

Yield:12 servings

Ingredients

- 1 cup creamy peanut butter (or other nut butter)
- 1/4 cup honey
- 1 teaspoon vanilla extract
- 2 medium ripe bananas, mashed
- 1/2 teaspoon salt
- 1 teaspoon ground cinnamon
- 2 1/4 cups quick oats

- 1/2 cup dried cranberries or raisins
- 2/3 cup chopped nuts, such as almonds, walnuts or pistachios

Instructions

Preheat the oven to 325°F. Line a baking sheet with parchment paper or a Silpat.

In the bowl of a stand mixer fitted with the paddle attachment, beat together the peanut butter, honey, vanilla extract, mashed bananas, salt, and cinnamon.

Add the oats, dried cranberries, and nuts and mix until combined. Scoop about 1/4-cup mounds of the cookie dough onto the baking sheet, flattening each cookie slightly. (The cookies will not spread while baking, so you can space them relatively close together.)

Bake the cookies for 14 to 16 minutes until they're golden brown but still soft. Remove the cookies from the oven then allow them to cool for 5 minutes on the baking sheet before transferring them to a rack to cool completely.

Crookpot Apple Cinnamon Oats

Total Prep Time: 7-8 hrs

Yield: 4 servings

Ingredients

- 2 gala apples peeled and diced
- 1/2 cup brown sugar
- 1 tsp cinnamon
- 1 tsp pure vanilla
- 2 cups rolled oats
- 5 cups unsweetened vanilla almond milk

Directions

Place diced apples in the bottom of your greased (You can spray with coconut oil) 3-quart slow cooker.

Sprinkle cinnamon, brown sugar, and vanilla on apples.

Add rolled oats to slow cooker.

Add unsweetened vanilla almond milk.

Set on low for 7-8 hours, or on high for 3-4 hours.

Stir if desired and enjoy

Blueberry Banana Muffins

Total Time:30 Min

Yield:12 Servings

Ingredients

Flax Egg

- 1 tbsp ground flaxseed
- 3 tbsp water

Muffins

- 2 cups spelled flour

- 2 tsp baking powder
- 1 tsp cinnamon
- 1/2 tsp baking soda
- 1/2 tsp salt

- 1 cup blueberries fresh or frozen
- 1 cup walnuts chopped
- 3 very ripe bananas peeled
- 1/4 cup maple syrup
- 1/4 cup coconut oil melted

Instructions

Preheat oven to 350°

Combine ground flaxseed and water in a small bowl, and allow to sit while you continue with the recipe.

Line a 12 cup muffin tin with liners, or use a non-stick muffin tin .

In a bowl, combine spelled flour, baking powder, cinnamon, baking soda, salt, blueberries, and walnuts.

In another bowl, mash bananas with a fork or potato masher

Add maple syrup, your flax egg, and coconut oil to the bananas, and combine

Add banana mixture to the dry ingredients, mixing quickly to just combine and moisten. Don't over mix.

Spoon mixture into muffins cups, dividing evenly.

Bake in center of the oven, about 20 minutes, or until a toothpick inserted in the center comes out clean.

Remove from oven, and cool on a wire rack .

25-Min Buckwheat Crepes

Total Time: 25 Minutes

Yield: 12 Servings

Ingredients

Crepes

- 1 cup un-toasted (raw) buckwheat flour
- 3/4 Tbsp flaxseed meal
- 1 3/4 cups light (canned) coconut milk
- 1 pinch sea salt
- 1 Tbsp avocado or melted coconut oil (plus a bit more for cooking // or use nonstick pan)
- 1/8th tsp ground cinnamon (optional // omit for savory)

- sweetener (optional // to taste // You can use a dash of stevia // omit for savory or unsweetened)

Fillings (Optional)

- Compote
- Nut Butter
- Coconut Whipped Cream
- Granola
- Cinnamon Baked Apples

Instructions

To a blender or mixing bowl, add buckwheat flour (see notes), flaxseed meal, light (canned) coconut milk, salt, avocado oil, cinnamon (omit for savory), and sweetener of choice (omit for savory or unsweetened).

Pulse in blender or whisk in mixing bowl to combine. The batter should be pourable but not watery. If too thin, add a bit more buckwheat flour. If too thick, thin with more dairy-free milk.

Heat a cast-iron or nonstick skillet over medium heat. (Non-stick is typically best for crepes, but You can use a seasoned cast-iron skillet and it worked well, too). Once hot, add a little oil and spread into an even layer. Let the oil heat until hot - when you flick a little water onto the pan, it should crackle and evaporate almost immediately.

Add ~1/4 cup (60 ml) batter. Let cook until the top appears bubbly and the edges are dry (similar to pancakes). Then carefully flip and cook for 2-3 minutes more on the other side. Turn heat down if cooking too quickly.

Repeat until all crepes are prepared. We didn't find we needed to add any more oil after the first crepe. Keep warm between layers of parchment paper or on a plate under a towel.

Serve as is with a little vegan butter, nut butter, maple syrup, compote, or other fillings or choice! My preferred is vegan butter, berries, maple syrup, and banana. But these would also be delicious with coconut whipped cream, Cinnamon Baked Apples, fresh fruit (e.g. berries or bananas), or granola.

Best when fresh, but you can store leftovers sealed in the refrigerator for up to 3 days. To freeze, layer between pieces of parchment paper (to prevent sticking) and freeze. Then store in a freezer-safe container up to 1 month. To reheat, warm in a 350-degree F (176C) oven or microwave until hot.

Multigrain Pancakes

Total Prep Time: 30 min

Yield:8-9 Servings

Ingredients

- 3 tbsp. butter, plus more for the skillet
- ½ cup whole wheat flour
- ½ cup all-purpose flour
- ¼ cup barley or rye flour
- 2 tbsp. sugar
- 1 tbsp. plus 1 tsp. baking powder
- ½ tsp. salt
- 2 large eggs
- 1 cup plain, full-fat yogurt

- 2 tbsp. milk, plus more as needed
- ½ tsp. lemon zest
- ½ tsp. vanilla extract
- About 1 cup blueberries (fresh or frozen)

Directions

Melt two tablespoons of the butter. Stir in the third tablespoon until it is completely melted. (This keeps the butter from being too warm when you add it to the other ingredients.) Set aside.

In a small bowl, combine the flours, sugar, baking powder, and salt. Whisk to blend. Set aside.

In a large bowl, combine the eggs, yogurt and milk and whisk together. If you are using a thin yogurt, no additional milk should be needed. If you use a thick yogurt such as Greek yogurt, add 1-2 more tablespoons of milk. Whisk in the melted butter, lemon zest, and vanilla. Add in the dry ingredients and whisk in just until incorporated.

Warm the oven to 200° F and have a baking sheet ready (to keep finished pancakes warm). Heat a skillet or sauté pan over medium heat and grease lightly with butter. Ladle about 1/3 cup of batter onto the cooking surface for each pancake. Dot the top with blueberries. Allow cooking until bubbles begin to form on the top surface. Use a large spatula to carefully flip the pancake and cook the other side until lightly golden and cooked through. Repeat with the remaining batter, storing finished pancakes in the oven until ready to serve.

Pumpkin Granola Yogurt Parfait

Total Prep Time:1 Hr

Yield:12 Servings

Ingredients

- 5 cups rolled oats (if you want to add chopped nuts (almonds, walnuts, pecans), do 3 cups of oats and 1 cup nuts instead)
- 1/2 tsp salt
- 1 1/2 tsp cinnamon
- 1 1/2 tsp pumpkin pie spice
- 1/2 cup honey
- 1/4 cup brown sugar
- 1/3 cup coconut oil, warmed to liquid form

- 2 tsp vanilla
- 3 Tbsp canned pumpkin
- Yoplait light Pumpkin Pie yogurt – You can use one 6 oz container to make 2 mini parfaits

Instructions

Preheat oven to 325 and lightly grease a large baking sheet with a raised edge.

In a large bowl, mix together the oats, salt, cinnamon and pumpkin pie spice.

In another bowl, whisk together the honey, brown sugar, coconut oil, vanilla, and canned pumpkin. Add the wet mixture to the oat mixture and stir until well combined.

Spread the mixture evenly onto the prepared baking sheet and bake for 15-minute intervals, stirring in between each interval. The granola is ready when all of it is golden brown and no longer moist (mine was ready after about 55 minutes).

Allow to cool completely and then layer the granola with Yoplait light Pumpkin Pie yogurt in single-serving dishes. Store any remaining granola in an airtight container for about a week.

Sweet Potato Oat Waffles

Total Time:15 Min

Yield: 8 Servings

Ingredients

- 2 cups Sweet potato puree or leftover sweet potato casserole or pumpkin puree.
- 2 Eggs
- 2 cups Oats gluten-free
- 2 tsp Baking powder
- 1 tsp Baking soda

- 1/2 tsp salt
- 1 tsp Cinnamon
- 1/2 tsp Nutmeg ground
- 1 cup Milk
- 1 tsp Vanilla extract--omit if using leftover casserole

Instructions

Grease and preheat the waffle iron according to manufacturer instructions.

Place all ingredients in a blender and blend until smooth and incorporated.

Ladle 1/3 cup of mixture unto each waffle iron mold and cook until golden on both sides.

Serve with toasted walnuts and maple syrup if desired.

Bread French Toast

Total Time: 15 Min

Yield: 4

Ingredients

- Bread – 2 slices
- 1 whole egg
- 2 oz egg whites
- Splash of Almond Milk
- Cinnamon or Pumpkin Pie Spice

Directions

Preheat a skillet on medium heat. Whisk 1 egg, 2 oz egg whites, a splash of almond milk and cinnamon or pumpkin pie spice (pumpkin pie adds more flavor). Soak 1 slice of Ezekiel Bread in french toast batter. Spray skillet with cooking spray. Add bread to pan and cook for 2 min on each side. Repeat with other slice of bread!

Breakfast Sandwich

Total Time: 14 Mins

Yield: 2 Servings

Ingredients

- 6 eggs
- 1 tablespoon milk
- 1 tablespoon butter
- 4 pieces cooked bacon
- 1/2 tomato diced
- 2 avocado

- 1/2 cup shredded cheese
- 2 English muffin
- salt and pepper
- cilantro for garnish optional

Instructions

Heat a skillet on medium heat and cook bacon until crisp and set aside and let drain on paper towels. Once cooled chop the bacon into bite small pieces.

In a small bowl mash up the avocado. Sprinkle with a little salt and pepper.

In another bowl whisk eggs and milk until combined, heat a skillet on medium-low add butter and let melt, add eggs and gently mix until scrambled about 1-2 minutes sprinkle with salt and pepper to taste.

Split English muffin with a fork and toast until lightly browned. Top with avocado, tomatoes and scrambled eggs, add cheese.

Place under broiler just until cheese melts about 1-2 minutes. Add chopped bacon and cilantro garnish...Enjoy!

Turkey Bacon & Egg Breakfast Tacos

Total Time: 45 Minutes

Yield: 6 Servings

Ingredients

- 1 large egg
- 3 large egg whites
- Splash of almond milk
- Salt and pepper, to taste
- 4 pieces of turkey bacon (or regular bacon)
- 2 tablespoons shredded cheddar cheese

- ½ cup cherry tomatoes, halved
- ½ avocado, cubed
- 4 white corn tortillas (taco-sized)
- Optional: cilantro for garnish

Instructions

First, preheat oven to 400ºF and line a baking sheet with tin foil. Place 4 strips of turkey bacon on a sheet and bake for around 15 minutes or until as crispy as you like it. Set aside.

In a small bowl, whisk together 1 egg, 3 egg whites, and a splash of almond milk.

Spray a nonstick pan with coconut oil cooking spray and heat to medium/high heat. Scramble eggs with a spatula and season with salt and pepper.

Separate the scrambled eggs onto 4 tortillas. Then, add a piece of bacon. Top with cherry tomatoes, cheese, avocado, and cilantro.

Tofu Scramble

Total Prep Time:30 Min

Yield:2 Servings

Ingredients

SCRAMBLE

- 8 ounces extra-firm tofu
- 1-2 Tbsp olive oil
- 1/4 red onion (thinly sliced)
- 1/2 red pepper (thinly sliced)
- 2 cups kale (loosely chopped)

SAUCE

- 1/2 tsp sea salt (reduce amount for less salty sauce)
- 1/2 tsp garlic powder
- 1/2 tsp ground cumin
- 1/4 tsp chili powder
- Water (to thin)
- 1/4 tsp turmeric (optional)

FOR SERVING (optional)

- Salsa
- Cilantro
- Hot Sauce
- Breakfast potatoes, toast, and/or fruit

Instructions

Pat tofu dry and roll in a clean, absorbent towel with something heavy on top, such as a cast-iron skillet, for 15 minutes.

While tofu is draining, prepare the sauce by adding dry spices to a small bowl and adding enough water to make a pourable sauce. Set aside.

Prep veggies and warm a large skillet over medium heat. Once hot, add olive oil and the onion and red pepper. Season with a pinch each salt and pepper and stir. Cook until softened - about 5 minutes.

Add kale, season with a bit more salt and pepper, and cover to steam for 2 minutes.

In the meantime, unwrap tofu and use a fork to crumble into bite-sized pieces.

Use a spatula to move the veggies to one side of the pan and add tofu. Sauté for 2 minutes, then add sauce, pouring it mostly over the tofu and a little over the veggies. Stir immediately, evenly distributing the sauce. Cook for another 5-7 minutes until tofu is slightly browned.

Serve immediately with the breakfast potatoes, toast, or fruit. I like to add more flavor with salsa, hot sauce, and/or fresh cilantro. Alternatively, freeze for up to 1 month and reheat on the stovetop or in the microwave.

2. Lunch Recipes

Veggie Quesadillas Recipe

Total Time: 15 min

Yield: 4 Servings

Ingredients

- 1 cup beans, black or pinto
- 2 Tablespoons cilantro, chopped

- ½ bell pepper, finely chopped
- ½ cup corn kernels
- 1 cup low-fat shredded cheese
- 6 soft corn tortillas
- 1 medium carrot, shredded
- ½ jalapeno pepper, finely minced (optional)

Cilantro Yogurt Dip

- 1 cup plain non-fat yogurt
- 2 Tablespoons cilantro, finely chopped
- Juice from ½ of a lime

Directions

1. Preheat large skillet over low heat.

2. Line up 3 tortillas. Divide cheese, corn, beans, cilantro, shredded carrots, and peppers between the tortillas.

3. Cover each with a second tortilla.

4. Place a tortilla on a dry skillet and warm until cheese is melted and tortilla is slightly golden about 3 minutes.

5. Flip and cook another side until golden, about 1 minute.

6. In a small bowl mix together the nonfat yogurt, cilantro and lime juice.

7. Cut each quesadilla into 4 wedges (12 wedges total) and serve 3 wedges per person with about ¼ cup of the dip.

8. Refrigerate leftovers within 2 hours.

Beet Arugula Pizza Recipe

Total Prep Time: 1hr 30 min

Yield:8 Servings

Ingredients

Pizza Crust

- 1 packet active dry yeast
- ¾ cup lukewarm water
- 2 cups 100% whole wheat flour
- 1 ½ teaspoons salt
- Oil for greasing the bowl

Pizza

- 2 small beets, roasted
- 1 cup arugula
- ½ cup goat cheese
- 1 cup blackberries
- 2 tablespoons honey
- 2 tablespoons balsamic vinegar

Directions

Pizza Crust

1. Pour warm water into a large bowl and sprinkle with yeast

2. Whisk the mixture and let sit until foamy, about 5 minutes

3. Add salt then slowly stir in flour until a sticky dough forms

4. Transfer dough to an oiled bowl, cover with plastic wrap, let sit ~1 hour in a warm corner of the kitchen to let rise

5. Knead the dough a few times, until the dough becomes sticky and begins to form a ball

6. Roll out dough and bake at 500 F for 8-12 minutes depending on the thickness of crust

Roasted Beets

1. While the dough is rising, dice beets

2. Place on a baking sheet lined with parchment paper

3. Cover with foil

4. Bake 35 minutes at 400 F

5. Once beets are finished roasting, increase oven temperature and bake pizza crust

Pizza

1. Top crust with roasted beets while the oven cools to 350 F

2. Sprinkle with goat cheese and berries

3. Drizzle with honey and balsamic vinegar

4. Bake 8-10 minutes at 350 F

5. Top with arugula

Chicken Wrap

Total Time: 45 Min

Yield:4 Servings

Ingredients

- 8 oz chicken breast (one large breast)
- ½ cup celery, diced
- 2/3 cup canned mandarin oranges, drained
- ¼ cup onion, minced
- 2 tablespoons mayonnaise
- 1 teaspoon soy sauce
- ¼ teaspoon garlic powder
- ¼ teaspoon black pepper

- 1 large whole wheat tortilla
- 4 large lettuce leaves, washed and patted dry

Directions

1. In a non-stick pan, cook chicken breast on medium-high heat until done throughout (internal temperature of 165°F). When the chicken has cooled enough to handle, cut into ½ inch cubes.

2. In a medium bowl, mix chicken, celery, oranges and onions. Add mayonnaise, soy sauce, garlic, and pepper. Mix gently until chicken mixture is evenly coated.

3. Lay tortilla on clean cutting board or large plate. With a knife or clean kitchen, scissors cut the tortilla into four quarters. Place 1 lettuce leaf on each tortilla quarter, trimming the leaf so it doesn't hang over the tortilla.

4. Put ¼ of the chicken mixture in the middle of each lettuce leaf. Roll tortillas up into a cone, with the two straight edges coming together and the curved edge creating the opening of the cone. Eat like a sandwich wrap.

5. Refrigerate leftovers within 2 hours.

Black Bean Cake Recipe

Total Time:45 Minutes

Yield:4 Servings

Ingredients

- 2 slices whole-wheat bread, torn
- 3 tablespoons fresh cilantro
- 2 cloves garlic
- 1 (15-ounce) can low sodium black beans, rinsed and drained
- 1 (7-ounce) can chipotle peppers in adobo sauce
- 1 teaspoon ground cumin
- 1 large egg
- ½ medium avocado, seeded and peeled
- 1 tablespoon lime juice

- 1 small plum tomato

Directions

1. Place was torn bread in food processor bowl or blender container. Cover and process or blend until bread resembles coarse crumbs. Transfer crumbs to a large bowl and set aside.

2. Process or blend cilantro and garlic until finely chopped. Add beans, 1 of the chipotle peppers, 1 to 2 teaspoons of adobo sauce, and cumin. Process or blend using on/off pulses until beans are coarsely chopped and mixture begins to pull away from sides.

3. Add mixture to bread crumbs in a bowl. Add egg and mix well.

4. Shape mixture into four ½-inch-thick patties. Grill on lightly greased rack of uncovered grill directly over medium heat for 8 to 10 minutes or until patties is heated through, turning once.

5. Meanwhile, for guacamole, in small bowl mash avocado. Stir in lime juice. Season with salt and pepper. Serve patties with guacamole and tomato.

Rice Bowl (SouthWest) Recipe

Total Time: 20 Min

Yield: 2 Servings

Ingredients

- 1 teaspoon vegetable oil
- 1 cup chopped vegetables (try a mixture - bell peppers, onion, corn, tomato, zucchini)
- 1 cup cooked meat (chopped or shredded)
- 1 cup cooked brown rice
- 4 tablespoons salsa
- 2 tablespoons shredded cheese

- 2 tablespoons low-fat sour cream

Directions

1. In a medium skillet, heat oil over medium-high heat (350 degrees in an electric skillet). Add vegetables and cook for 3 to 5 minutes or until vegetables are tender-crisp.

2. Add cooked meat, beans or tofu and cooked rice to skillet and heat through.

3. Divide rice mixture between two bowls. Top with salsa, cheese, sour cream and serve warm.

4. Refrigerate leftovers within 2 hours.

Salmon Salad Pita

Total Time: 10 Min

Yield:3 Servings

Ingredients

- ¾ cup canned Alaskan salmon
- 3 tablespoons plain fat-free yogurt
- 1 tablespoon lemon juice
- 2 tablespoons red bell pepper, minced
- 1 tablespoon red onion, minced
- 1 teaspoon capers, rinsed and chopped
- Pinch of dill, fresh or dried
- Black pepper to taste

- 3 lettuce leaves
- 3 pieces small whole wheat pita bread

Directions

1. Mix the first 8 ingredients together in a small bowl to make a salmon salad.

2. Place 1 lettuce leaf and 1/3 cup salmon salad inside each pita.

Stuffed Portobello Mushroom Caps

Total Time: 17 min

Yield:1 Servings

Ingredients

- 2 portobello mushroom caps
- 1 small Roma tomato, diced
- 2 tablespoons pesto
- ¼ cup shredded low-fat mozzarella cheese

Directions

1. Use a dry or damp cloth to clean mushrooms. Remove stems by twisting gently.

2. Divide pesto evenly between 2 mushroom caps.

3. Top with diced tomato and shredded cheese.

4. Bake in oven for 15 minutes at 400 F.

Tuna Salad Recipe

Total Prep Time: 15 min

Yield: 2 Servings

Ingredients

- 5 oz can light tuna in water, drained
- 1 tablespoon extra virgin olive oil
- 1 tablespoon red wine vinegar
- ¼ cup chopped green onion tops
- 2 cups arugula
- 1 cup cooked pasta (from 2 oz dry)
- 1 tablespoon freshly shaved parmesan cheese
- black pepper

Directions

1. In a large bowl toss tuna with oil, vinegar, onion, arugula, and cooked pasta.

2. Divide between two plates and top with parmesan and pepper.

3. Serve immediately.

Shrimp Rolls Recipe

Total Time: 20 Min

Yield: 6 Servings

Ingredients

- 12 sheets of rice paper
- 12 bib lettuce leaves
- 12 basil leaves
- ¾ cup fresh cilantro
- 1 cup carrots, shredded
- ½ medium cucumber, thinly sliced

- 1 ¼ pound (20 ounces) shrimp, cooked, deveined and peeled

Directions

1. Wash and prepare lettuce, basil, cilantro, carrots and cucumber.

2. Lay all vegetables and shrimp out on the counter assembly-line style for easy access.

3. Lay a damp paper towel down on a clean cutting board. Run one sheet of rice paper under warm water until just wet and place on paper towel.

4. Layer 1 lettuce leaf, 1 basil leaf, 1 Tablespoon cilantro, carrots and cucumber on the rice paper at the end closest to you. Carefully begin to roll the rice paper over the vegetables like you would a burrito.

5. When the vegetables are just covered, place about 4 shrimp on the rice paper. Continue rolling the rice paper up like a burrito, don't forget to tuck in the ends before it's all wrapped up.

6. Repeat the process until all 12 rolls are made. Serve immediately.

Apple Turkey Gyro

Total Time: 10 Min

Yield: 6 Servings

Ingredients

- 1 tablespoon vegetable oil
- 1 cup onion, sliced
- 1 cup sweet red pepper, thinly sliced
- 1 cup sweet green pepper, thinly sliced
- 2 tablespoons lemon juice
- ½ pound cooked a turkey or chicken breast, cut into thin strips

- 1 apple (cored), preferably Golden Delicious; sliced or finely chopped
- 6 whole-wheat pocket pita bread, warmed
- ½ cup low fat or fat-free plain yogurt

Directions

1. In large skillet, heat oil over medium heat. Add onion, peppers, and lemon juice and cook until tender.
2. Stir in turkey and apple and cook until turkey is heated through. Remove from heat. Fill each pita with some of the mixtures; drizzle with yogurt. Serve warm.

Pizza Pita

Total Time: 10 min

Yield:2 Servings

Ingredients

- 2 pieces whole wheat pita bread
- ½ cup grated reduced sodium mozzarella cheese
- ¼ cup pizza or tomato sauce
- Veggies of choice: mushrooms, bell pepper, onion, olives, artichoke hearts, etc

Directions

1. Preheat oven or toaster oven to 350 degrees. Split the pita bread halfway around the edge and spoon in the cheese, tomato sauce, and any toppings.

2. Wrap the pita in aluminum foil and bake for 7 to 10 minutes or until cheese melts.

Turkey & Cheese Sandwich

Total Time: 7 Min

Yield: 2 Servings

Ingredients

- 2 slices multi-grain or rye sandwich bread
- 2 tsp Dijon-style mustard
- 2 slices (1 oz. each) reduced-sodium cooked or smoked turkey
- 1 USA pear, cored and thinly sliced
- 1/4 cup shredded low-fat mozzarella cheese
- Coarsely ground pepper

Directions

1. Spread each slice of bread with 1 teaspoon mustard. Place one slice turkey on each slice of bread. Arrange pear slices on turkey and sprinkle each with 2 tablespoons cheese. Sprinkle with pepper.

2. Broil, 4 to 6 inches from heat, 2 to 3 minutes or until turkey and pears are warm and cheese melts. Cut each sandwich in half and serve open face.

Heartfelt Tuna Melt

Total Time: 5 Min

Yield: 4 Servings

Ingredients

- 6 ounces white tuna packed in water, drained
- 1/3 cup chopped celery
- 1/4 cup chopped onion
- 1/4 cup low fat Russian or Thousand Island salad dressing
- 2 whole-wheat English muffins, split
- 3 ounces reduced-fat Cheddar cheese, grated
- Salt and black pepper to taste

Directions

1. Preheat broiler.

2. Combine tuna, celery, onion and salad dressing. Season with salt and pepper.

3. Toast English muffin halves. Place split-side-up on a baking sheet and top each with 1/4 of tuna mixture. Broil 2-3 minutes or until heated through.

4. Top with cheese and return to broiler until cheese is melted, about 1 minute longer.

Spinach, Mushroom & Mozzarella Wraps

Total Time: 10 Minutes

Yield: 2 Servings

Ingredients

- 1 tablespoon olive oil
- 8 oz. fresh mushrooms, sliced (about 2 ½ cups)
- 1 teaspoon minced garlic
- 2 whole wheat 8" tortillas

- ½ pound fresh spinach or arugula, trimmed and steamed
- 1 plum tomato, diced
- ¼ cup (1 ounce) shredded part-skim mozzarella cheese

Directions

1. Preheat oven to 350°F. Heat 1 tbsp olive oil in sauté pan over high heat. Add a single layer of mushrooms and garlic. Leave the mushrooms alone as they sauté – be patient as they turn red-brown – then turn and sauté until the second side turns a similar color.

2. On each tortilla arrange layers of spinach, tomato, mozzarella, and cooked mushrooms. Roll up and place seam-side down in a lightly oiled baking dish. Bake uncovered until hot and cheese is melted, about 10 minutes.

3. Cut each tortilla crosswise into quarters. Serve warm or room temperature as desired.

Apple-Swiss Panini

Total Time: 3-5 Minutes

Yield: 4 Servings

Ingredients

- 8 slices whole-grain bread
- ¼ cup non-fat honey mustard
- 2 crisp apples, thinly sliced
- 6 ounces low-fat Swiss cheese, thinly sliced
- 1 cup arugula leaves
- Cooking spray

Directions

1. Preheat panini press on medium heat. If you don't have a panini press, just use a non-stick skillet.

2. Lightly spread honey mustard evenly over each slice of bread. Layer apple slices, cheese, and arugula leaves over 4 slices of bread. Top each with remaining bread slices.

3. Lightly coat panini press with cooking spray. Grill each sandwich for 3 to 5 minutes or until cheese has melted and bread has toasted. Remove from pan and allow to cool slightly before serving.

Grilled Veggie Sandwich

Total Time: 10 Min

Yield: 4 Servings

Ingredients

- 3 tablespoons light mayonnaise
- 3 cloves garlic, minced
- 1 tablespoon lemon juice
- 1/8 cup olive oil
- 1 cup red bell peppers, sliced
- 1 small zucchini, sliced
- 1 red onion, sliced

- 1 small yellow squash, sliced
- 2 slices focaccia bread

Directions

1. In a bowl, mix the mayonnaise, minced garlic, and lemon juice. Set aside in the refrigerator.

2. Preheat the grill for high heat.

3. Brush vegetables with olive oil on each side. Brush grate of grill with oil. Place bell peppers and zucchini closest to the middle of grill, and set onion and squash pieces around them. Cook for about 3 minutes, turn and cook for another 3 minutes. The peppers may take a bit longer. Remove from grill and set aside.

4. Spread some of the mayonnaise mixtures on cut sides of bread; sprinkle each with feta cheese. Place on the grill, cheese side up, and cover with a lid for 2 to 3 minutes. Watch carefully so the bottoms don't burn.

5. Remove bread from grill and layer with vegetables. Enjoy as open-faced grilled sandwiches.

Vegetable Pasta Soup

Total Time:~ 35 Minutes

Yield:12 (3/4-Cup) Appetizer Servings

Ingredients

- 2 teaspoons olive oil
- 6 cloves garlic, minced
- 1 1/2 cups coarsely shredded carrot
- 1 cup chopped onion
- 1 cup thinly sliced celery
- 1 32-ounce box reduced-sodium chicken broth

- 4 cups of water
- 1 1/2 cups dried ditalini pasta
- 1/4 cup shaved Parmesan cheese

Directions

1. In a 5- to 6-quart Dutch oven, heat oil over medium heat. Add garlic; cook for 15 seconds. Add carrot, onion, and celery; cook for 5 to 7 minutes or until tender, stirring occasionally. Add chicken broth and the water; bring to boiling. Add uncooked pasta; cook for 7 to 8 minutes or until pasta is tender.

2. To serve, top individual servings with Parmesan cheese and parsley. Makes 12 (3/4-cup) appetizer servings.

Tuna Salad

Total Time:~ 10 Minutes

Yield:4 (1 Cup Each) Servings

Ingredients

- 2 6-ounce cans chunk light tuna, drained
- 1 15-ounce can small white beans, such as cannellini or great northern, rinsed (see Ingredient note)
- 10 cherry tomatoes, quartered
- 4 scallions, trimmed and sliced
- 2 tablespoons extra-virgin olive oil

- 2 tablespoons lemon juice
- 1/4 teaspoon salt

Directions

1. Combine tuna, beans, tomatoes, scallions, oil, lemon juice, salt and pepper in a medium bowl. Stir gently. Refrigerate until ready to serve.

Delicious Tortellini Salad

Total Prep Time:~ 2hr 10 Minutes

Yield: 8 Main-Dish Servings

Ingredients

- 1 9-ounce package refrigerated light cheese tortellini or ravioli
- 3 cups broccoli florets
- 1 cup crinkle-cut or sliced carrots (2 medium)
- 1/4 cup sliced green onions (2)
- 1/2 cup bottled reduced-fat ranch salad dressing
- 1 large tomato, chopped
- 1 cup fresh pea pods, halved

Directions

1. In a large saucepan cook pasta according to package directions. Add the broccoli and carrots during the last 3 minutes of cooking. Drain. Rinse with cold water. Drain again.

2. In a large bowl combine the cooked pasta mixture and green onions; drizzle with dressing. Gently toss to coat. Cover and chill for 2 to 24 hours.

3. Before serving, gently stir tomato and pea pods into pasta mixture. If necessary, stir in a little milk to moisten. Makes 8 main-dish servings.

Melon, Strawberry & Avocado Salad

Total Time:~ 20 Minutes

Yield: 4 Servings

Ingredient

- 1/4 cup honey
- 2 tablespoons sherry vinegar, or red-wine vinegar
- 2 tablespoons finely chopped fresh mint
- 1/4 teaspoon freshly ground pepper

- Pinch of salt
- 4 cups baby spinach
- 1 small avocado, (4-5 ounces), peeled, pitted and cut into 16 slices
- 16 thin slices cantaloupe, (about 1/2 small cantaloupe), rind removed
- 1 1/2 cups hulled strawberries, sliced
- 2 teaspoons sesame seeds, toasted

Directions

1. Whisk honey, vinegar, mint, pepper, and salt in a small bowl.

2. Divide spinach among 4 salad plates. Arrange alternating slices of avocado and cantaloupe in a fan on top of the spinach. Top each salad with strawberries, drizzle with dressing and sprinkle with sesame seeds.

3. Dinner Recipes

Vegetables & Turkey Stir-Fry

Total Time: 20 Minutes

Yields: 8 servings

Ingredient

- 1 tablespoon oil
- ½ teaspoon salt
- Thin slices ginger root, minced

- 1 clove garlic, peeled and minced or 1/8 teaspoon garlic powder
- 1 cup turkey, cut into ½-inch cubes
- 2 cups chopped vegetables, fresh, frozen or canned, such as celery, mushrooms, water chestnuts, bok choy
- ½ teaspoon sugar
- 3 cups cooked brown rice

Directions

1. Heat oil in a large skillet over medium heat. Add salt, ginger root, garlic, turkey and vegetables. Stir-fry for 1 minute. Reduce heat to prevent scorching. Add sugar.

2. When vegetables are tender, remove pan from heat. If vegetables are firm, add 1-2 tablespoons of water cover and cook for 2 more minutes or until tender. Serve over rice (or noodles). Refrigerate leftovers within 2-3 hours.

White Beans & Shrimp Recipe

Total Time: 12 Min

Yields:4 Servings

Ingredient

- 2 tablespoons olive oil
- 1 pound large shrimp, peeled and deveined
- 1 medium onion, chopped
- 4 cloves garlic, minced
- 2 teaspoons chopped fresh sage
- 2 tablespoons balsamic vinegar
- ½ cup low sodium, fat-free chicken broth

- 15 ounce can no-salt-added cannellini beans, rinsed and drained
- 5 cups baby spinach
- 1 ½ ounce crumbled reduced-fat feta cheese

Directions

1. Heat 1 teaspoon oil in a large non-stick skillet over medium-high heat. Cook shrimp until just opaque, about 2 to 3 minutes. Transfer to a plate.

2. Heat remaining oil in the same skillet over medium-high heat and add onion, garlic, and sage; cook 4 minutes stirring occasionally until golden. Stir in vinegar and cook 30 seconds.

3. Add broth, bring to a boil and cook 2 minutes. Stir in beans and spinach and cook until the spinach wilts, about 2 to 3 minutes. Remove from heat and stir in shrimp. Top with feta cheese and divide among 4 bowls.

Turkey Fajitas Bowls

Total Time: ~10 Min

Yields: 4 Servings

Ingredients

- 1/2 pound turkey breast
- 2 tablespoons olive oil
- 1 tablespoon lemon juice
- 1 clove Garlic, crushed
- 3/4 teaspoon fresh chile pepper, or dried to taste
- 1/2 teaspoon dried oregano leaves
- 1/2 large yellow bell pepper, cut into 1-inch pieces
- 1/2 large green pepper, cut into 1-inch pieces

- 1 medium tomato, cut into 12 wedges
- 1/2 cup shredded cheddar cheese for topping
- 4- 8" corn tortillas or Make your own tostada bowls

Directions

1. Cut turkey into thin slices and then into strips about 3/4 inch wide. In a medium bowl, combine 1 tablespoon of the oil with the lemon juice, garlic, fresh Chile pepper, and oregano. Add turkey and stir to coat. Let marinate for 1/2 hour.

2. Heat remaining 1 tablespoon oil in a nonstick skillet over medium-high heat. Add yellow and green peppers, stir fry 2 minutes. Add turkey strips and stir fry another 3 minutes. Stir in tomato and heat.

3. Warm tortillas in a skillet and use it as a base. Fill the tortilla or tostada bowl and top with cheese and salsa.

Baked Sweet Potatoes

Total Time: 1hr

Yield:4 servings

Ingredients

- 4 medium-sized sweet potatoes
- ½ cup fat-free Greek yogurt (or light sour cream)
- 1 teaspoon low sodium taco seasoning
- 1 teaspoon olive oil
- 1 red pepper, diced (about ½ cup)
- ½ red onion, diced (about ½ cup)
- 1 teaspoon chili powder
- ½ teaspoon paprika
- ½ teaspoon cumin

- A pinch of salt
- 1 1/3 cups canned reduced-sodium black beans, rinsed and drained
- ½ cup reduced-fat Mexican cheese blend
- ¼ cup chopped scallions or cilantro
- ½ cup salsa (optional)
- 4 tablespoons salsa for topping

Directions

1. Poke holes in the potato with a fork, cook on your microwave's potato setting until potatoes are soft and cooked through (about 8-10 minutes on high for 4 potatoes). If you don't have a microwave, bake in the oven for about 45 minutes at 400°F.

2. Combine yogurt and taco seasoning in a small bowl, mix well.

3. Heat oil in a medium pot over medium heat. Add peppers, onions, chili powder, paprika, cumin, and salt; cook until the onions have caramelized slightly, about 5 minutes.

4. Add black beans, stir to combine and heat through (about another 5 minutes).

5. Slice the potato lengthwise down the middle or use a fork to pierce the skin.

6. Top with 2 tbsp shredded cheese, 1/3 cup of black bean mixture, 2 tbsp Greek yogurt mixture and 2 tbsp of salsa.

Tandoori Chicken

Total Prep Time: ~ 45 Min

Yields: 6 Servings

Ingredient

- 1 cup plain nonfat yogurt
- ½ cup lemon juice
- 5 garlic cloves, crushed
- 2 tbsp paprika
- 1 tsp yellow curry powder
- 1 tsp ground ginger

- 1 tsp crushed hot red pepper flakes (use ½ tsp for a milder flavor)
- 6 skinless, boneless chicken breasts cut into 1-2 inch pieces
- 6 skewers soaked in water for at least 15 minutes

Directions

1. Preheat oven to 400 degrees F. Combine yogurt, lemon juice, garlic, paprika, yellow curry powder, ginger and red pepper flakes in a blender and process until smooth.

2. Skewer an equal amount of chicken pieces onto each of the soaked skewers. Place chicken skewers in a shallow casserole dish. Add half of the yogurt mixture, reserving the remainder. Cover and chill for about 15 minutes.

3. Spray another shallow baking dish with cooking spray. Remove chicken skewers, discard the yogurt marinade, and place chicken skewers in prepared dish. Brush chicken with reserved yogurt mixture.

4. Bake for 15-20 minutes or until juices run clear when meat is pierced. Serve immediately. For a slightly more authentic preparation grill, the chicken skewers over medium-high heat for 3-5 minutes per side.

Poblano Peppers(Stuffed)

Total Time: 30 Min

Yield: 4 Servings

Ingredient

- 4 large poblano peppers
- ½ cup uncooked brown rice
- 1 ½ cups Fresh Grilled Salsa or other low-sodium salsa
- 1 15-ounce can black beans
- 1 ½ cup of frozen corn
- 1 teaspoon cumin
- 1 teaspoon chili powder

- 1/8 teaspoon cayenne pepper
- Freshly ground black pepper to taste
- ½ cup 2% Mexican blend cheese, shredded

Directions

1. Cook rice according to package instructions.

2. Slice each poblano pepper in half lengthwise and remove the seeds and ribs.

3. Place the peppers in a baking dish skin side up. Broil for 3-5 minutes and then flip over the peppers and broil 3-5 minutes longer. Watch the pepper closely to make sure they only char and don't overly burn.

4. Drain and rinse the black beans. In a large, microwave-safe bowl, combine the beans, salsa, corn, a quarter cup of cheese, cumin, chili powder, and cayenne. Add pepper to taste. Heat the filling for about 2-3 minutes in the microwave, or until warm, stirring after each 30-second increment. Stir in the rice.

5. Spoon the filling into each pepper half. Top with the remaining cheese and broil until the cheese is melted, about 2 minutes longer. Serve immediately.

Pork With Apples & Sweet Potatoes

Total Prep Time: 30 Min

Yield: 4 Servings

Ingredients

- ¾ cup apple cider
- ¼ cup apple cider vinegar
- 2 tablespoons maple syrup
- ¼ teaspoon smoked paprika
- 1 teaspoon grated fresh ginger or ¼ teaspoon dried ginger
- 1 teaspoon ground black pepper
- 2 teaspoons vegetable oil

- 1 – 12-ounce pork tenderloin
- 1 large sweet potato- cut into ¼ to ½-inch cubes
- 1 large apple- cut into ½- inch cubes

Directions

1. Preheat the oven to 375°.

2. In a medium bowl, combine apple cider, apple cider vinegar, maple syrup, smoked paprika, ginger, and black pepper; set aside.

3. Heat oil over medium-high heat in a large Dutch oven or large ovenproof sauté pan with a lid. Once the oil begins to smoke, reduce heat to medium and gently place the pork tenderloins in a pan. Cook, turning until all sides are well browned, about 8 to 12 minutes. Remove pan from the heat.

4. Place the sweet potatoes around the pork and pour apple cider mixture over the pork tenderloin. Cover and bake for 20 minutes. Roast until an instant-read thermometer inserted into the thickest part of the tenderloin registers 145 – 150°.

5. Turn sweet potatoes and place the apple quarters around the pork. Bake, uncovered for another 5 to 10 minutes, or until tenderloin registers 170°. Remove pork, apples, and sweet potatoes from roasting pan. Let the pork stand for 10 minutes before slicing.

6. As pork rests, reduce cider mixture to about a ¼ cup. Slice roasted pork into ½ thick medallions, serve with the sweet potatoes and apples, and pour cider reduction over everything on the plate.

Spaghetti Squash Lasagna

Total Time: 50 Min

Yield: 4 servings

Ingredients

- 2 cups marinara sauce
- 3 cups roasted spaghetti squash (1 large spaghetti squash)
- 1 cup part-skim ricotta
- 8 teaspoons grated parmesan cheese
- 6 ounces part-skim shredded mozzarella
- Crushed red pepper or ground pepper to taste

Directions

1. To roast spaghetti squash: Cut the squash in half lengthwise, scoop out the seeds and fibers with a spoon. Place on a baking sheet, cut side up and sprinkle with salt and pepper. Bake at 350 degrees for about an hour, or until the skin gives easily under pressure and the inside is tender. Remove from the oven and let it cool 10 minutes. Using a fork, scrape out the squash flesh a little at a time. It will separate into spaghetti-like strands. Measure 3 cups for a lasagna recipe. Drain off any excess liquid.

2. Preheat oven to 375 degrees. Spread 1 cup of marinara sauce onto the bottom of the baking dish. Top evenly with roasted spaghetti squash. Next, layer the ricotta cheese and sprinkle with half of the parmesan and mozzarella. Add the remaining sauce and finish with the remaining parmesan and mozzarella. Sprinkle with pepper.

3. Cover with foil and bake for 15 – 20 minutes, or until the cheese is melted and the edges begin to bubble; uncover and cook an additional 5 minutes.

Tortilla Bake

Total Time: 15Min

Yield: 4 Servings

Ingredients

- 8 corn tortillas, cut in half
- 1 cup shredded Monterey Jack cheese
- 1 cup fresh or frozen corn
- 1 cup cooked black or pinto beans
- 2 green onions, sliced
- 3 eggs
- 1 cup fat-free milk

- 1/2 teaspoon chili powder
- 1 4-ounce can diced green chilies
- 1 tomato, sliced
- Salsa

Directions

1. Preheat oven to 350 degrees.

2. Coat an 8-inch square baking dish with non-stick spray or oil. Arrange 5 tortilla halves to cover the bottom of the pan. Top with 1/3 cup each of the cheese, corn, and beans. Sprinkle with 1/2 of the green onions. Arrange another 5 tortilla halves on top to cover and top with 1/3 cup cheese, the remaining corn, beans and green onions. Arrange the last 5 tortilla halves over the top to cover.

3. In a medium bowl add eggs, milk and chili powder; whisk to combine. Stir in the green chilies. Pour the egg and milk mixture over the tortillas evenly. Top with tomato slices and the remaining 1/3 cup cheese.

4. Bake, uncovered until a knife inserted into the center comes out clean, about 50 minutes. Let stand for 10 minutes at room temperature before serving. Serve warm with salsa.

Chicken Pesto Bake

Total Time: ~10 Min

Yield: 4 Servings

Ingredients

- 2 (160 ounces total) boneless, skinless chicken breasts
- 4 teaspoons basil pesto
- 1 medium tomato, sliced thin
- 6 tablespoons shredded reduced-fat mozzarella cheese
- 2 teaspoons grated parmesan cheese

Directions

1. Wash the chicken and pat dry with a paper towel. Slice the chicken breast horizontally to create 4 thinner pieces.

2. Preheat the oven to 400 degrees Fahrenheit. Line a baking sheet with foil or parchment.

3. Place the chicken on the baking sheet and spread 1 teaspoon of pesto onto each piece of chicken.

4. Bake for 15 minutes or until the chicken is no longer pink in the center. Remove from the oven and top with tomatoes, mozzarella, and parmesan cheese.

5. Return to the oven for another 3 to 5 minutes or until the cheese is melted.

Shrimp Pasta Primavera

Total Prep Time: 15 Minutes

Yield: 6 Servings

Ingredients

- 1-1/4 cup fresh asparagus, sliced into 1-inch lengths (about 1/2 pound)
- 12 ounces whole-wheat penne pasta
- 1 cup green peas, fresh or frozen
- 2 tsp olive oil
- 1 tbsp garlic, minced
- 1/8 tsp crushed red pepper

- 1 pound medium shrimp, peeled and deveined (thawed if frozen)
- 1/2 cup green onion, thinly sliced
- 2 tsp fresh lemon juice
- 1 tbsp fresh parsley, chopped
- 1/3 cup grated Parmesan cheese
- 1/2 tsp salt
- Fresh ground black pepper

Directions

1. Bring a 6-quart pot of water to a boil. Add asparagus and cook until tender-crisp, about 4 minutes. Transfer to a bowl with a slotted spoon. Add the pasta and cook according to the package directions. In the last 2 minutes of cooking, add the peas. Drain the pasta with the peas and reserve in the bowl with the asparagus.

2. Meanwhile, heat the olive oil in a 12-inch nonstick skillet over medium heat. Add the minced garlic and crushed red pepper and cook, stirring, until fragrant, about 1 minute. Add the shrimp and cook for about 2 minutes on each side. Add the pasta with the vegetables, green onion, lemon juice, parsley, and Parmesan cheese. Toss to coat and season with salt and fresh ground black pepper to taste.

Shepherd's Pie

Total Time: 25 Min

Yield:6 Servings

Ingredients

- 2 large baking potatoes, peeled and diced
- 1/2 cup low-fat milk
- 1 pound lean ground beef
- 1 medium onion, chopped
- 1 clove garlic, minced
- 2 tablespoons flour
- 4 cups of frozen mixed vegetables
- 3/4 cup reduced-sodium beef broth

- 1/2 cup shredded cheddar cheese
- ground pepper to taste

Directions

1. Put diced potatoes in a saucepan; add enough water to barely cover. Bring to boil. Reduce heat and simmer, covered, until soft (about 15 minutes).

2. Drain potatoes and mash. Add milk, and set mixture aside.

3. Preheat oven to 375 degrees.

4. Brown meat, onion, and garlic in a large skillet. Stir in flour, and cook for 1 minute, stirring constantly.

5. Add vegetables and broth. Cook 5 minutes until bubbly. Stir well.

6. Spoon vegetable mixture into an 8-inch square baking dish. Spread potato mixture over vegetable/meat mixture. Sprinkle cheese on top.

7. Bake 25 minutes, until hot and bubbly.

8. Refrigerate leftovers within 2-3 hours.

Sesame-Honey Chicken & Quinoa Bowl

Total Time: 10-14 Minutes

Yield: 4 Servings

Ingredients

Quinoa & Carrot Slaw

- 1 1/2 cups water
- 3/4 cup quinoa, rinsed
- 2 cups grated carrots (about 3 large)
- 2 tablespoons rice vinegar

- 2 tablespoons sesame seeds, toasted
- 1 tablespoon sesame oil

Sesame-Honey Chicken

- 2 tablespoons sesame oil
- 2 cups cooked chicken breast, cut into bite-sized pieces
- 3 tablespoons honey
- 3 tablespoons reduced-sodium soy sauce
- 2 tablespoons water
- 1 teaspoon cornstarch
- 2 scallions, sliced

Directions

1. To prepare quinoa: Bring 1 1/2 cups water to a boil in a small saucepan. Add quinoa and return to a boil. Reduce to a low simmer, cover and cook until the water is absorbed 10 to 14 minutes. Uncover and let stand.

2. To prepare carrot slaw: Meanwhile, combine carrots, rice vinegar, sesame seeds, and 1 tablespoon oil in a medium bowl. Set aside.

3. Combine sesame oil, honey, soy sauce, 2 tablespoons water and cornstarch in a small bowl. Pour into a medium skillet. Cook over medium heat, stirring, until the sauce has thickened. Add chicken and stir until coated with sauce, about 1 minute.

4. Divide the quinoa among 4 bowls and top each with 1/2 cup carrot slaw and 3/4 cup chicken mixture. Sprinkle with scallions.

Sesame Noodles & Chicken

Total Time: 40 Min

Yield: 8 Servings

Ingredients

- 8 ounces whole-wheat spaghetti noodles
- 12 ounces frozen broccoli florets
- 1/4 cup vegetable oil
- 1 tablespoon minced garlic
- 1 1/2 cup cooked, diced chicken breast (8 ounces)
- 2 tablespoons sugar
- 3 tablespoons low sodium soy sauce
- 2 tablespoons rice vinegar
- 1 tablespoon toasted sesame seeds

Directions

1. Cook pasta according to package directions. Set aside.

2. Mix together sugar, soy sauce, and vinegar in a small bowl. Set aside.

3. Heat oil in large sautés pan or skillet. Add garlic and broccoli and cook on medium until soft.

4. Add chicken and cook until heated through.

5. Add pasta and soy sauce mixture, and mix well. Sprinkle sesame seeds on top.

6. Refrigerate leftovers within 2-3 hours.

Baked Chicken Tenders

Total Time: 12 Min

Yield: 4 Servings

Ingredients

- 16 ounces chicken tenderloins
- 2 teaspoons sesame oil
- 2 teaspoons low sodium soy sauce
- 6 tablespoons toasted sesame seeds
- ½ teaspoon coarse salt
- 4 tablespoons panko breadcrumbs (no salt added)
- olive oil spray

Directions

1. Preheat over to 425 degrees F and spray a baking sheet with non-stick oil spray or parchment paper.

2. Combine the sesame oil and soy sauce in a bowl. Combine the sesame seeds, salt, and panko in another bowl.

3. Place the chicken in the bowl with the oil and soy sauce, then into the sesame seed mixture to coat well.

4. Place this on the baking sheet; lightly spray the top of the chicken with oil spray and bake 8-10 minutes. Turn over and cook another 4-5 minutes longer or until cooked through.

Salsa Verde Burger

Total Time: 35Min

Yield: 4 Servings

Ingredients

Burger

- Cooking spray
- pinch of pepper
- 4 (93% lean) beef patties, 4.75 ounces each
- ½ cup salsa verde
- 4 slices reduced-fat pepper jack cheese
- 4 (100 calories) whole-wheat hamburger buns

- ¼ cup shredded red cabbage
- 4 ounces sliced of avocado

Salsa Verde

2 tomatillos

- 1 serrano chile pepper, sliced
- ¼ cup onion, sliced
- ¼ teaspoon chopped garlic

Directions

1. Place the tomatillos, Serrano peppers, onion, and garlic in a saucepan. Add water to just cover and bring to a boil then reduce the heat to medium-low and cook until the tomatillos are soft and have turned slightly brownish in color, about 20-30 minutes.

2. Add more water if needed to keep the mixture from burning as it cooks.

3. Pour the cooked vegetables into a blender and blend until smooth.

4. Heat a skillet or grill over high heat.

5. When hot, spray with cooking spray and add the patties.

6. Season with pepper and cook a few minutes on each side, to your desired liking.

7. Add the cheese and cover; cook to melt, about 30 seconds.

8. Place the cooked burgers on the buns and top each burger with 2 tablespoons salsa verde, red cabbage, and avocado slices.

Quinoa Spinach Patties

Total Time: 40 Min

Yield: 7 Servings

Ingredients

- 1 cup uncooked quinoa
- 4 eggs, whisked
- 1/3 cup parmesan cheese
- 3 large scallions, sliced thin
- 3 cloves garlic, minced
- 1 cup steamed spinach, chopped (frozen is fine)
- 1 cup whole-wheat breadcrumbs

- 1 teaspoon olive oil
- 2 cups of water

Directions

1. Rinse the quinoa thoroughly then place the quinoa in a medium saucepan with 2 cups of water. Bring the water to a boil then reduce it to a simmer. Cook until the quinoa is tender and has absorbed the liquid, about 20 minutes. Let it cool.

2. In a large bowl, combine the quinoa, eggs, parmesan, scallions, garlic, steamed spinach, and breadcrumbs. Let everything sit for a few minutes to absorb the liquid. The batter should be moist, but not runny. Form patties of ¼ cup each.

3. Heat oil in a large non-stick skillet over medium-low heat. In 2 or 3 batches, cook the patties, covered, for 8-10 minutes on each side, or until browned and golden. Makes 14 patties.

Delicous Chili

Total Time: 13 Min

Yield:7 Servings

Ingredients

- 1/2 pound lean ground meat
- 1/2 medium onion, chopped
- 1 can (15.5 ounces) kidney beans, drained
- 1 can (14.5 ounces) diced tomatoes with liquid
- 1 1/2 tablespoons chili powder

Directions

1. Brown meat and onions in a large skillet over medium-high heat (350 degrees in an electric skillet). Drain fat.

2. Add beans, tomatoes, and chili powder.

3. Reduce heat to low (250 degrees in an electric skillet), cover and cook for 10 minutes.

4. Serve hot.

5. Refrigerate leftovers within 2-3 hours.

Salmon With Mustard-Dill Sauce

Total Time: 15 Min

Yield: 4 Servings

Ingredients

- 1 teaspoon olive or vegetable oil
- 2 tablespoon shallots, finely chopped
- 1 1/2 cup fat-free or low-fat milk
- 1/2 teaspoon salt
- Freshly ground black pepper to taste

- 1 1/4 lb salmon fillet, about 1 inch thick, skin on, cut into 4 portions
- 1 tablespoon fresh lemon juice
- 1 1/2 teaspoons cornstarch
- 2 tablespoons chopped fresh dill
- 1/4 cup reduced-fat sour cream
- 2 teaspoons Dijon mustard
- Lemon wedges and fresh dill sprigs for garnish

Directions

1. In a 10-inch skillet or sauté pan, heat oil over medium heat. Add shallots and sauté until softened, 30 to 60 seconds. Add milk, shallots, salt, and pepper; bring to simmer, stirring. Reduce heat to low.

2. Slip salmon pieces in the milk sauce, skin-side up; immediately turn over. Cover and poach salmon gently, spooning milk cooking liquid over top of salmon occasionally, just until interior is opaque, 10 to 12 minutes.

3. With a slotted spoon, carefully transfer salmon to a warm platter. Cover with foil and keep warm.

4. In a small bowl, mix lemon juice and cornstarch; add to poaching liquid and cook, stirring constantly, until slightly thickened, about 1 minute. Stir in sour cream, chopped dill and mustard.

5. Garnish salmon with lemon wedges and dill sprigs. Serve with the mustard-dill sauce.

Stuffed Turkey & Vegetables

Total Time: 50 Minutes

Yield: 6 Servings

Ingredients

- 1 cup cooked brown rice
- 3 bell peppers (green, red, or yellow)
- 10 oz ground turkey
- 1 tsp Italian seasoning (or basil and oregano leaves)
- 1/2 tsp garlic powder
- 1/4 tsp each salt and pepper
- 1/2 onion
- 1 cup sliced mushrooms

- 1 chopped zucchini (about 1 cup)
- 1 can (14.5 oz) diced tomatoes with liquid

Directions

1. Cook the rice or prepare instant rice according to package directions. Preheat oven to 350 degrees.

2. In a large skillet over medium heat, cook the turkey until no longer pink. Add seasonings during the last few minutes. Add onion, mushrooms, and zucchini to the skillet. Saute until tender. Mix in tomatoes and rice. Remove from heat.

3. Cut the peppers in half from top to bottom. Remove the stem and seeds. Place pepper halves in a baking dish and fill with the skillet mixture. Cover the baking dish with foil. Bake at 350 degrees for 40 to 50 minutes or until peppers is tender when poked with a fork.

4. Refrigerate leftovers within 2 to 3 hours.

4. Desserts Recipes

Fresh Strawberries With Yogurt

Total Time: 5 Min

Yield: 4 Servings

Ingredients

- 1 pint fresh strawberries
- 4 teaspoons honey

- 3 cups plain low-fat yogurt
- 4 Tablespoons toasted sliced almonds

Directions

1. Clean and slice strawberries into quarters, set aside.

2. Place ¾ cup of yogurt into each of 4 serving dishes. Divide the strawberries evenly among the dishes. Top each with 1 teaspoon honey and 1 tablespoon toasted sliced almonds. Serve immediately.

Pumpkin Pie

Total Time: 50 Min

Yield: 8 Servings

Ingredients

- 1 cup ginger snaps
- 16 ounces canned pumpkin
- 1/2 cup egg whites
- 1/2 cup sugar
- 2 teaspoons pumpkin pie spice
- 12 ounce can evaporate skim milk

Directions

1. Preheat oven to 350. Grind the cookies in a food processor. Lightly spray a 9" glass pie pan with vegetable cooking spray. Pat the cookie crumbs into the pan evenly.

2. Mix the rest of the ingredients in a medium-sized mixing bowl. Pour into the crust and bake until a knife inserted in center comes out clean, about 45 minutes.

3. Store in the refrigerator. Allow to cool and slice in 8 wedges.

Tahini & Almond Cookies

Total Time: 12-14 Minutes

Yield: 54 servings

Ingredients

- 1 cup unbleached white flour
- 1 cup + 2 tablespoons whole wheat flour
- 2/3 cup almond meal
- ½ cup + 3 tablespoons cold unsalted butter, cut into cubes
- ¾ cup of sugar

- 1 teaspoon vanilla extract
- Pinch of salt
- 2 tablespoons water
- ¾ cup + 2 tablespoons tahini paste

Directions

1. Preheat oven to 350°F. Line two baking sheets with parchment paper.

2. In a food processor, blend unbleached white flour, whole wheat flour, almond meal, butter, sugar, vanilla, and salt. Process until the mixture looks crumbly.

3. Add water and tahini, process until a smooth dough forms.

4. Remove dough from the food processor and knead it a few times on the counter until smooth (if the dough feels very dry, dampen your hands and knead the dough slightly).

5. Create small balls of the dough, place them on the baking sheet, then flatten each one slightly with your fingers.

6. Bake 12-14 minutes, or until golden brown.

7. Cool completely and serve.

Fruit Skewers with Cheesecake

Total Time: 7 Min

Yield: 24 Servings

Ingredients

Cheesecake Dipping Sauce:

- 4 ounces 1/3 less fat cream cheese (Neufchatel), softened
- 1 cup fat-free Greek yogurt
- 1 teaspoon vanilla extract
- ¼ cup of sugar

Skewers:

- 14 ounces angel food cake, cut into 1-inch cubes

- 72-84 medium strawberries (about 3 ½ pounds), stems removed
- 1-pint blueberries
- 24 skewers

Directions

1. In a medium bowl, combine the cream cheese with yogurt, vanilla, and sugar. Mix well until sugar dissolves. Set aside.

2. Thread 3 strawberries and 2 cubes of cake onto each skewer, alternating between strawberries and cake. Finish each skewer with 3 blueberries. Place finished skewers on a platter. Refrigerate skewers and dip until ready to eat.

Chocolate Chip Cookies

Total Time: 30 Min

Serves: 5

Ingredients

- 2 cups rolled oats (not quick-cooking)
- 1/2 cup all-purpose flour
- 1/2 cup whole-wheat pastry flour
- 1 teaspoon ground cinnamon
- 1/2 teaspoon baking soda
- 1/2 teaspoon salt
- 1/2 cup tahini 4 tablespoons cold unsalted butter, cut into pieces
- 2/3 cup granulated sugar

- 2/3 cup packed light brown sugar
- 1 large egg
- 1 large egg white
- 1 tablespoon vanilla extract
- 1 cup semisweet or bittersweet chocolate chips
- 1/2 cup chopped walnuts

Directions

1. Position racks in the upper and lower thirds of the oven; preheat to 350°F. Line 2 baking sheets with parchment paper or Silpat silicone liners.

2. Whisk oats, all-purpose flour, whole-wheat flour, cinnamon, baking soda and salt in a medium bowl.

3. Beat tahini and butter in a large bowl with an electric mixer until blended into a paste. Add granulated sugar and brown sugar; continue beating until well combined-the mixture will still be a little grainy. Beat in egg, then egg white, then vanilla. Stir in the oat mixture with a wooden spoon until just moistened. Stir in chocolate chips and walnuts.

4. With damp hands, roll 1 tablespoon of the batter into a ball, place it on a prepared baking sheet and flatten it until squat, but don't let the sides crack. Continue with the remaining batter, spacing the flattened balls 2 inches apart.

5. Bake the cookies until golden brown, about 16 minutes, switching the pans back to front and top to bottom halfway through.

6. Cool on the pans for 2 minutes, then transfer the cookies to a wire rack to cool completely. Let the pans cool for a few minutes before baking another batch.

7. Store in an airtight container for up to 2 days or freeze for longer storage

Milk Chocolate Pudding

Top pudding with sliced bananas or strawberries to add a serving of fruit to your dessert.

Total Time: 7 Min

Yield: 4 Servings

Ingredients

- 3 tablespoons cornstarch
- 2 tablespoons cocoa powder
- 2 tablespoons sugar
- 1/8 teaspoon salt
- 2 cups nonfat milk

- 1/3 cup chocolate chips

Directions

1. In a medium saucepan, mix cornstarch, cocoa powder, sugar, and salt until well combined. Whisk in milk. Heat over medium, stirring frequently, until thickened and just beginning to bubble.

2. Remove from heat; stir in chocolate chips and vanilla until chocolate chips are melted and the pudding is smooth.

3. Pour into 4 serving dishes or one large dish and chill until set. To prevent a skin from forming on top place plastic wrap on the surface of the pudding.

Maccerated Berries with Frozen Yogurt

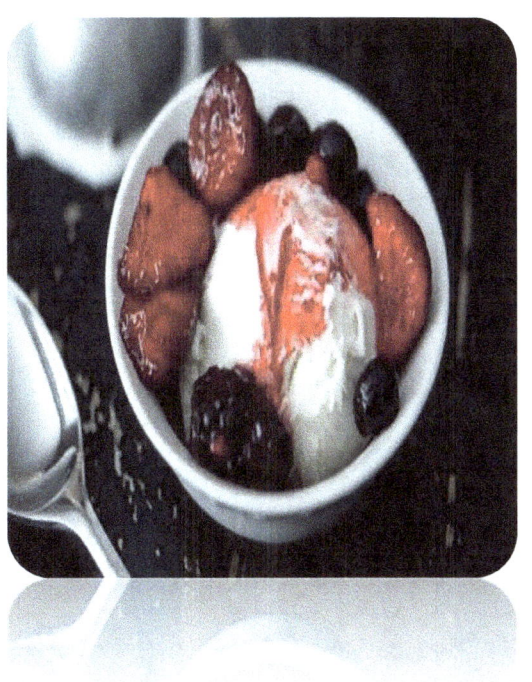

Total Time: 2 hrs

Yield: 4 Servings

Ingredients

- 1 cup strawberries, sliced
- 1 cup fresh blueberries
- 1 cup fresh raspberries
- 1 tablespoon sugar
- 1 teaspoon freshly grated orange zest

- 3 tablespoons fresh orange juice
- 1-pint low-fat vanilla or plain frozen yogurt

Directions

1. Combine the berries and sugar in a large bowl.

2. Using a fine grater, remove 1 teaspoon of zest from the fresh orange. Add the zest to the berries.

3. Slice the same orange in half and squeeze. Add 3 tablespoons of the orange juice to the berries. Toss to combine.

4. Chill for at least 2 hours or overnight.

5. Place 1/2 cup of low-fat frozen yogurt into each of 4 dessert bowls. Top each scoop with macerated berries.

Pear-Strawberry Trifle

Total Time: 4 hr 20 Min

Yield: 10 Servings

Ingredients

- 2 pared, cored, and thinly sliced pears
- 2 tablespoons lemon juice
- 2 cups coarsely chopped strawberries
- ½ teaspoon almond extract, optional
- 2 tablespoons orange juice
- 2 tablespoons honey
- ½ 9 inch angel food cake, cut to 1-inch cubes
- 3 cups vanilla or lemon-flavored yogurt

- Garnish: pear slices and mint sprigs

Directions

1. Toss pears in lemon juice, and strawberries in almond extract (if using).

2. Combine orange juice and honey, mix well.

3. Layer a deep 2 to 2 ½ quart glass bowl in the following order: 1/3 of cake sprinkled with 1 tablespoon orange juice mixture, 1 cup yogurt, 1 cup pear slices, 1 cup strawberries; repeat.

4. Layer remaining cake, sprinkle with remaining orange juice mixture and spread 1 cup yogurt over top. Cover with plastic wrap and refrigerate 1 to 4 hours before serving.

5. Garnish with pear slices and mint just before serving.

Lactose-Free Chocolate Pudding

Total Time: 25 Minute

Yield: 8 Servings

Ingredients

- 4 cups low-fat lactose-free milk
- ¼ cup cornstarch
- ¼ cup unsweetened cocoa powder, preferably Dutch-processed
- ¼ teaspoon kosher salt
- 2 ounces unsweetened chocolate, coarsely chopped

- ¼ cup plus 2 tablespoons sugar
- 1 teaspoon pure vanilla extract

Directions

1. In a small bowl, blend ½ cup of milk with the cornstarch.

2. In a heavy saucepan combine the cocoa and salt; slowly whisk in the remaining 3 ½ cups milk, the chocolate, and the sugar. Heat over moderate heat, stirring occasionally, until the chocolate is melted.

3. Whisk in the cornstarch mixture. Cook, stirring frequently, over very low heat until very thick and just beginning to boil, about 10 minutes.

4. Remove from the heat and stir in the vanilla extract. Let cool, stirring occasionally until the custard is just warm.

5. Pour the pudding into individual ½-cup custard cups or small bowls. Cover with plastic wrap and refrigerate until chilled and set.

Carrot Cake Cookies

Total Time: 38 Minutes

Yield: 48 Servings

Ingredients

- 1/2 cup packed light-brown sugar
- 1/2 cup sugar
- 1/2 cup oil
- 1/2 cup applesauce or fruit puree
- 2 eggs
- 1 teaspoon vanilla
- 1 cup flour
- 1 cup whole wheat flour

- 1 teaspoon baking soda
- 1 teaspoon baking powder
- 1/4 teaspoon salt
- 1 teaspoon ground cinnamon
- 1/2 teaspoon ground nutmeg
- 1/2 teaspoon ground ginger
- 2 cups old-fashioned rolled oats (raw)
- 1 1/2 cups finely grated carrots (about 3 large carrots)
- 1 cup raisins or golden raisins

Directions

1. Preheat oven to 350 degrees.

2. Mix sugars, oil, applesauce, eggs, and vanilla thoroughly.

3. Stir dry ingredients together.

4. Blend dry ingredients into the wet mixture. Stir in raisins and carrots.

5. Drop by teaspoonful on greased cookie sheet.

6. Bake 12-15 minutes until golden brown.

7. Store in an airtight container.

Almond Rice Pudding

Total Time: 5 Min

Serves: 1

Ingredients

- 3 cups of milk
- 1 cup white rice
- 1/4 cup sugar
- 1 teaspoon vanilla
- 1/4 teaspoon almond extract
- cinnamon to taste

- 1/4 cup toasted almonds — optional

Directions

1. Combine milk and rice in a medium saucepan, and bring to a boil.

2. Reduce heat and simmer for 1/2 hour with the lid until the rice is soft.

3. Remove from heat and add the sugar, vanilla, almond extract, and cinnamon.

4. Sprinkle toasted almonds on top and serve warm.

5. Refrigerate leftovers within 2-3 hours.

Tips:

Try using brown rice instead of white to for extra fiber. This yummy dessert contributes ½ cup toward your daily goal of 3 cups milk.

Watermelon Sorbet

Total Time: 5 min

Serves: 1

Ingredients

- 8 cups cubed (1 inch) watermelon, seeds and rind discarded
- 1 cup simple sugar syrup
- 2 tablespoons fresh lemon juice

Directions

Puree the watermelon cubes in a food processor. Measure 4 cups of the puree and place in a bowl. Add the Simple Sugar Syrup, lemon juice and stir well. Freeze in an ice cream maker according to the manufacturer's instructions.

Conclusion

The DASH Diet is very effective for managing high blood pressure. It also help in promoting a healthier lifestyle, as it focuses mainly on the consumption of healthy food items (vegetables, grains, fruits, lean meats, and low-fat dairy).

Thank you so much for securing a copy of my cookbook. I believe you have gotten adequate ideas for healthy DASH dieting recipes. Eating healthy doesn't have to be tasteless, boring or difficult. It can be tasty and fun!

Eat Healthy, Stay Healthy!